PSALM 91

PRAYER OF PROTECTION FROM EVIL ATTACKS

GRACE REMMY

CONTENTS

INTRODUCTION

The Bible is the only weapon in which believers use to fight and proclaim formidable victory over the enemies. Without the Bible, there can never be victory and our prayers become useless and the devil would begin to take the glory.

One of the powerful scriptures against night raiders, spiritual attacks and prayers that guarantee a peaceful sleep, is a prayer from the book of Psalm 91.

We live in a wicked world today, and the devil is not getting any kinder. Every believer that must survive the attacks of darkness must be giving to intense prayers and spiritual understanding of the word.

The bible talks about the snare of the fowler, (psalm 91:3), this means the traps of the enemy. The devil is busy setting all manner of traps for believers, for instance, relationship traps, many Christians are trapped in wrong marriages and with the wrong people, there are also ancestral traps, where believers are struggling with ancestral powers and demonic forces.

The bible also talks about the terror, by night, the arrow by day, and the pestilence that roam in darkness, this is different spiritual attacks that are thrown to believers from the pits of hell.

This evil is carried by satanic agents and demonic people, that is why you see people die of witchcraft attacks and strange sicknesses, sicknesses that cannot be detected through a medical diagnosis.

This psalm 91 prayer points for protection, will help you as you prayerfully build a wall of protection over your life.

- From today, no devil or demonic agents shall prevail over your life in Jesus name.
- Pray this prayer in faith today and see divine protection in your life in Jesus' name.

CHAPTER 1

THE PRAYER OF PSALM 91

The book of psalms is a powerful and all-purpose prayer book. Every believer that wants to see the raw manifestation of God in his/her prayer life must take advantage of the book of psalms.

The book of psalms 91 is a prayer for protection psalm.

As believers, we must always be on guard and not allow the devil or his human agents take us by surprise.

Psalm 91 is a loaded gun when it comes to spiritual protection. Through Psalm 91, a lot of powerful prayer points for protection can be derived. in this book, I shall be dishing out powerful psalm 91 prayer points for protection for you.

Psalm 91 is a protection Scripture that believers have turned to for thousands of years whenever there is danger. As the Times of Trouble is upon us, the prayer of Psalm 91 is comforting and effective when prayed from the heart by those who love God and are in a relationship with Him.

Psalm 91 may be the most important passage of Scripture for the Days of Revelation ahead. The reality of supernatural protection is paramount for the times of supernatural events on the horizon. Faith is not the last resort, but a first response!

Psalm 91 is the answer to so many people's night prayers before bedtime. Although, there are other verses of the Bible that has the capacity to bind, cast, hijack and recover your blessings. But for the purpose of this teaching, we are focusing on the entire Psalm 91:1-16.

The word of God has influence and authority. Nothing can summon His command, stop or match it. Are you reading this message with pain and sorrow flowing in your heart, and likewise you noticed there is a battle going on against you?

Anywhere you go, you notice that there is a blockage? You are feeling like the more you pray the more the problems and the rage of the enemies against you.

Well, I want to let you know that there is hope for you, in Jesus' name.

There are lots of hidden divine powers embedded in Psalm 91. These hidden powers must be revealed to you.

Use the script of Psalm 91 and make it personal by changing the pronouns. God watches over His Word to perform it, so praying Psalm 91 from an "I" or "We" perspective is very effective. Praying this way puts you in the very middle of that truth and power.

If you have not prayed Scripture before, this may seem a little odd. Hang in there anyway. It is a prayer of proclamation, a proclamation of faith. This form of prayer is very different from the prayer of supplication or request. It provides a whole new point of view.

Memorize your prayer so that it is available to you (in your heart) when you need it most!

TAKE THE FOLLOWING PRAYERS:

- Almighty Father, I commit my life into your hands, please keep me in your secret place. Please keep me where the hand of the enemy cannot touch me, in the name of Jesus.
- Lord, my life is in your hands, please be my refuge and my fortress in the name of Jesus.
- Almighty Father, I pray that a thousand of my enemies may fall at my side, and ten thousand at my right hand; but it shall not come near me in Jesus name.
- No weapon formed against me shall prosper and every tongue that rises up against me in judgment shall be condemned in Jesus mighty name.
- Most High God, my life is in your hand, please be my defense. Protect me when I go out, protect me when I come in, protect me all the days of my life in the name of Jesus.

CHAPTER 2

MEANING OF PSALM 91

Psalm 91 King James Version (KJV)

1. He that dwelleth in the secret place of the Most High shall abide under the shadow of the Almighty.

2 I will say of the LORD, He is my refuge and my fortress: my God; in him will I trust.

3 Surely he shall deliver thee from the snare of the fowler, and from the noisome pestilence.

4 He shall cover thee with his feathers, and under his wings shalt thou trust: his truth shall be thy shield and buckler.

5 Thou shalt not be afraid for the terror by night; nor for the arrow that flieth by day;

6 Nor for the pestilence that walketh in darkness; nor for the destruction that wasteth at noonday.

7 A thousand shall fall at thy side, and ten thousand at thy right hand; but it shall not come nigh thee.

8 Only with thine eyes shalt thou behold and see the reward of the wicked.

9 Because thou hast made the LORD which is my refuge, even the most High, thy habitation;

10 There shall no evil befall thee, neither shall any plague come nigh thy dwelling.

11 For he shall give his angels charge over thee, to keep thee in all thy ways.

12 They shall bear thee up in their hands, lest thou dash thy foot against a stone.

13 Thou shalt tread upon the lion and adder: the young lion and the dragon shalt thou trample under feet.

14 Because he hath set his love upon me, therefore will I deliver him: I will set him on high, because he hath known my name.

15 He shall call upon me, and I will answer him: I will be with him in trouble; I will deliver him and honour him.

16 With long life will I satisfy him and shew him my salvation.

- The power behind Psalm 91 prayers are as follows: first, it makes you untouchable by the enemy.
- Second, it goes to heaven to order the angels to protect you.
- Third, it gives you peace of mind and guarantees your victory.

The prayer of the Psalmist is the prayer of deliverance. Until you understand this mysterious fact, ignorance will keep you in the place of church doctrine.

 The Bible says, "And Jabez called on the God of Israel saying, 'Oh, that You would bless me indeed, and enlarge my territory, that Your hand would be with me, and that You would keep me from evil, that I may not cause pain. ' So God granted him what he requested." (1 Chronicles 4:10).

This was a prayer of Jabez. He knew something was going wrong with him. The Bible says, God granted his request.

Psalm 139:22- **''I hate them with perfect hatred: I count them, mine enemies.''**

This Psalm is full of promises of blessings and protection for those who trust in the Lord. It makes believers have the belief that they are dwelling in the presence of God.

 As a believer, there is no need to fear "the terror of the night," nor the illness, nor the danger.

Verse 10 says that no evil will come to him, nor will any calamity come to his home.

This does not mean that you will never encounter difficulties or problems. It means that when someone trusts in the Lord, even bad things bring him closer to God.

 The greatest calamities, and even death itself, bring us closer to the eternal inheritance in Christ Jesus. All things cooperate for the good of those who love God.

God responds and God cares, God blesses those who make Him His shield. He even sends his angels to serve us. But do not think that by reciting this Psalm or having an open Bible on this page there will be some mystical power that will change your life.

What will change your life forever will be that you live in the shelter of the Lord. You must make your abode in God.

Believe in Jesus and the Holy Spirit will inhabit you and so you can live in the shelter of the Most High. You will live in God!

Unfortunately, so many believers have tried fruitlessly to overcome dark powers through prayers of the day, prayers of the night and through the word of God, but those prayers have remained abortive and ineffective before the Almighty God.

 On the other hand, they find themselves laboring so much in the place of prayers. They made several prayer strategies, but heavens say NO.

One of the major reasons why praying from the word of God goes unanswered is a result of sin.

The Bible says, your iniquities have separated his glory from you (Isaiah 59:2).

The seed of sin in the life of a believer can make a mockery of his or her prayers.

Therefore, whenever you are taking the prayer of Psalm 91 against the wicked, it is important as a prayer believer to repent and confess your sin or else, you will become helpless and God would not be able to fight your battles despite using the prayers from the book of Psalm or other scriptures.

It is highly rewarding to have continuous passion for prayers and the word of God. It is a good effort to channel your attention on prayers.

God loves a prayerful person. He loves to answer the prayers of a righteous person.

 Somebody asked: Why would God allow his children to suffer unto death?

The simple answer to this is taken from the book of James 1:12.

James 1:12, **"Blessed is the man that endureth temptation: for when he is tried, he shall receive the crown of life,**

which the Lord hath promised to them that love him."

God is ready to support and protect you whenever you pray but the problem is that a lot of people are praying under the foundation of wickedness, anger, pollution, envy, bitterness, immorality, etc.

No matter how prayerful you maybe, but it will be very difficult for you to get good answers from God – The Father, The Son, and The Holy Ghost when your life is obsessed with sin.

There are various powerful verses in Psalms. These types of Psalms are wonderful.

They include:

- A psalm of complaints (Psalm 3),
- Thanksgiving Psalm (Psalm 67).
- Royal Psalms (Psalm 18:50),
- Wisdom Psalms (Psalm 1, Psalm 37).
- Hymn Psalms (Psalm 8, 104, 148).

The Bible teaches us that genuine deliverance prayer is "more effective and dangerous than hypocritical prayers (Isaiah 29:11, James 5:6).

Indeed our prayers from the mind or scriptures are going to be "tested by fire". God does not look at prayers and answer them immediately.

He must look at the righteousness of the person. All believers are in constant spiritual warfare with the power of darkness.

But most of us fail to address our weaknesses. The Psalmist says, O God arise, and let my enemies be scattered, is one of the most important verses that encourage God to fight your battles.

The above verses make it clear until God appears in our troubles, all prayers involving binding, casting, nullifying, destroying will be a vain prayer effort.

I pray for you today, may your prayers never been in vain, in Jesus' name.

If Psalm 91 is one of your favorite scriptures then you should not stop. The simple truth is, the enemy does not want you to pray. The enemy does not want you to progress in the service of God. The enemy does not want you to recognize the particular portion in the book of Psalm that will bring massive protection to you.

 Do you know that if you notice your destiny prayers through Psalms, the devil is in trouble?

The Bible says, When David combined God's mercy with his divine power through prayers, he was confident that God would see him through his problems.

The book from Psalm 91 teaches us the prayer of protection or covering and also reminds us to stay in His presence, for it's a permanent place of testimony.

Reading Psalm 91 like a daily confession that gives you a big edge over the devil and his host. There is nothing the devil has done that God (word of God) cannot undo.

There are no challenges that Psalm 91:1-14 cannot handle effectively. It was the book of Psalm that recorded all the activities of David where God came out and fought against his troubles and setbacks that confronts him.

The Bible says, Psalm 34:21, ''Evil shall slay the wicked: and they that hate the righteous shall be desolate.''

It is crucial and important that you grow spiritually and be more sensitive.

Because, in the physical and spiritual realm, anybody can be a suspect.

That's why you need to be more prayerful this season. The power of God in the book of Psalm 91 cannot flow through in life so many people.

Because heaven is no longer in support of such prayers. God's miracles in the book of Psalm 91 cannot manifest when you are operating under a curse or covenant.

If you take the prayer of Psalm 91 wrongly, it may open the doors of troubles to you.

TAKE THE FOLLOWING PRAYERS:

- God prepare the instruments of death against my enemies, In the name of Jesus.
- Angels of God, arise and surround me with your wings of protection and power, in Jesus' name.
- Let calamity, tragedy, and afflictions fall upon the head of the strongman against my existence, in Jesus' name.
- The power that says, I will not experience peace until I die, O God, destroy them by fire, in Jesus' name.
- When others are attacked, the power of God will be my defense, in the name of Jesus.
- Every arrow, shot into my life from under-any water through witchcraft, come out of me and go back to your sender, in the name of Jesus.
- Any material taken from my body and now placed on a witchcraft altar, be roasted by the fire of God, in Jesus' name.
- Any drop of my blood sucked by any witch, be vomited now, in the name of Jesus.

- Any part of me shared out amongst household village witches, I recover you, in the name of Jesus.
- Let them begin to grope in the daytime as in the thickness of a dark night, in the name of Jesus.
- Let as many of them that are stubbornly unrepentant, be smitten by the sun in the day and by the moon, in the night in Jesus' name.
- Every evil image carved in my name, catch fire, in the name of Jesus.

CHAPTER 3

THE INTERPRETATION OF PSALM 91 MEANING

THE SECRET PLACE

Psalm 91:1 **"He that dwelleth in the secret place of the Most High shall abide under the shadow of the Almighty."**

Dwelling in the secret place of the Most High means a lot. The secret place means a hidden place.

A place where mysteries are being revealed.

Dwelling in the secret place means a person is hidden under divine protection and safety.

The secret place can also symbolize a place of rest, transformation, peace, etc.

To dwell means to live in a specified area. And that specified place is the heavenly place.

The Bible says, Acts 7:49, **"Heaven is my throne, and earth is my footstool: what house will ye build me? saith the Lord: or what is the place of my rest?"**

Dwelling in the secret place is specially designed for the righteous believers. God has a secret place for His own (Psalm 27:5, 31:20), and it is a place to live in.

Those who dwell there abide under the shadow of the Almighty, knowing His protection, comfort, and care.

The above verse can also mean that whatever you are doing in your most humble place shall be announced by God.

It is a beautiful thing for believers to dwell in the place of the Most High, because one of the advantages is that heaven will keep their watch over you.

God's promise of protection is conditional—it is realized only by those who draw close to him and do the work of the Father who is sitteth in heavenly places.

This involves more than just praying and fasting; Dwelling in the secret place means a time of profit, the reward for your persecution and steadfastness.

No wonder the Bible says, Matthew 11:28, **"Come unto me, all ye that labor and are heavily laden, and I will give you rest."**

 Abiding under the shadow of the Almighty are those people who are enjoying divine inheritance.

There are many people who seem to be faithful in everything especially in the areas of service to God, unfortunately, they are not abiding under the shadow (covering) of the Almighty.

The reason is largely due to sin and other negative attitudes. Until you dwell in the secret place of heaven, there will be no divine favor and intervention.

 The habit of living a humble and obedient life can make you receive speedy answers from God. Moses dwelleth in the secret place by going to bush and pray.

The Bible says the angel of the Lord appeared to him in flames of fire from within a bush (Exodus 3).

Moses built a prayer contact with heaven and he was protected. In Acts, people are being healed under the shadow of Peter (Acts 5:15).

If truly people were healed under Peter's shadow, then what can we expect under the shadow of the Lord?. To be close to God, you must be far from this world and the sin thereof.

 So, someone who abides in the secret place lives in the house of the Lord. The shadow of the Almighty represents divine recognition, power, and longevity.

For a Christian to abide under His shadow is not an easy thing. To get the attention of heaven towards your situation is even harder. But when you are finally hidden under his arms, there are several people who will be seeking to dethrone you.

Many things can be known as dwelling in the secret place of the Almighty God such as the following:

- Daily confession of your sin.
- Reading your Bible each day.
- Join a church fellowship and worship there continuously.
- Living a decent and moderate life.
- Treat others with love, charity, and forgiveness.
- Sharing the gospel of Christ, having a special place for prayers and admonitions.
- Relying constantly on the Holy Spirit.
- Learn the secret of recognizing the voice of God.

There is nothing the Almighty GOD wants us to do for Him that is not possible through His grace. His grace is sufficient for us.

For example, when he commits a task for us, He 'll be pleased to see us achieving the results of His plans towards us.

The grace of God is what is needed to keep dwelling in the secret place of our prayers despite the troubles of life.

Submission to the will of God is the secret to receiving and enjoying all the privileges given to us by our heavenly Father.

Daniel was an example of a person dwelling in the secret place of prayers. During his 21 days fasting, his prayers went up to the second heavens which prompted the devil to send a principality to hinder that prayer.

But he kept praying until God had to send the angels to release his blessings to him. God has done more than just promise protection.

In Bible times, he demonstrated this in miraculous ways that he is able to protect his people from demonic and witchcraft oppression of the day and night.

Dwelling in the secret place and abide under the shadow of the Almighty is a deep statement. When you are dwelling in the secret place, no devil can harm you. When you are dwelling in the secret place, no powers will take back the glory.

When you are dwelling in the secret place, you will be assured of His divine presence towards you.

When you are dwelling in the secret, the devil cannot bounce on your bed while asleep and oppress and suppress your life and destiny.

 In addition, God will make sure you are hidden from demonic attacks and summoning.

When your adversaries are calling your names in a cauldron, instead of you to appear, it is the raw fire from heaven that will blast your enemies to death, in Jesus' name.

So dwelling and abiding under God's hand is safer and more comfortable.

In Psalm 105:15, ''Touch not mine anointed and do my prophet no harm'' is a true confirmation that no demons will be able to kill you and lock you in satanic prison.

TAKE THE FOLLOWING PRAYERS:

- Unchangeable Lord, please don't let me be a prey in the mouth of the wicked in the name of Jesus.
- Let all the powers encamping against my goodness and breakthroughs become confused and be scattered, in the name of Jesus.
- Let all the powers of my adversaries be rendered impotent, in the name of Jesus.
- Let every evil tongue uttering curses and other evil pronouncements against my life be completely silenced, in the name of Jesus.
- I command every evil stronghold and powers housing my rights and goodness to be violently overthrown, in the name of Jesus.

CHAPTER 4

GOD IS MY REFUGE

Psalm 91:2- **"I will say of the Lord, He is my refuge and my fortress: my God; in him will I trust."**

The word refuge means, protection from danger. Refuge means, an escape from trouble.

While fortress means a defender from external attacks. It also means a secure place for safety and resting.

The above verses are the words of the psalmist, expressing his faith in the Lord for protection and comfort.

God has provided a truly remarkable demonstration of his protective power when he says He is our Refuge and Fortress.

Psalm 91 is a powerful word of personal confession written by Psalmist to guarantee our safety from the constant evil attacks that trouble our lives and destiny.

Being our refuge and fortress means He is our Redeemer. The Bible is an amazing offer that God makes to everyone to read, study and to warfare in the spirit realm.

By daily meditation of Psalm 91, it's divine virtues rested upon it protects us from sickness, financial shortage, depression, worry, fear, and stress.

It is, therefore, comforting that the Bible refers to God as our Refuge (2 Samuel 22:3) says: **"The God of my rock; in him will I trust: he is my shield, and the horn of my salvation, my high tower, and my refuge, my savior; thou savest me from violence." He is a mighty God with incredible capabilities.**

As the Lord of hosts and our Mighty man in battle, He is mighty to deliver and mighty to save.

It takes faith and confidence to believe that truly God is our only savior. For example, if you are given to fear, the effect of this verse upon your life may not come to pass.

 Irrespective of what you may be passing through right now, trust in God and call upon His name today, and He will give you all-round peace.

 The promise of" He is my refuge and fortress: My God; in him will I trust" is amazing and this does not mean that we are not going to experience any more battles after the confession.

No, our God does not guarantee us a problem-free life. He wants us to pass through some series of persecution before the light of healing will come to us.

Many people face severe adversities, including poverty, war, sickness, and death. But the Bible says, Psalm 46:1, God is our refuge and strength, a very present help in trouble.

 That is why Jesus stressed the need for protection from troubles and evil operations. Do you know that there are some people who don't believe in their prayers? Do you also know that Psalm 91 prayer of protection works very well for most people especially at night?

Have you ever asked yourself while the Psalmist prayers are not saving you from the problem of life? Maybe your pastors have given you some portion of Psalms to take for one fasting or the other and you simply gave up.

Knowing God as our refuge enables us to trust Him more freely. Knowing God as our fortress prevents us from the stronghold of the wicked.

When God is in charge of the situation, fear is taking away. **"The name of the LORD is a fortified tower; the righteous run to it and are safe"** (Proverbs 18:10).

David was a great example of someone who knew God as his refuge and fortress. He was a man of faith and confidence. At different points in his life, David was on the run from people who literally wanted to kill him, but he always found safety in God.

"My salvation and my honor depend on God; he is my mighty rock, my refuge. Trust in him at all times, you people; pour out your hearts to him, for God is our refuge" (Psalm 62:7–8).

My God in him I trust means so many symbols. First, it talks about faith. Second, it talks about endurance. Third, it explains more of casting your hope on God.

A person who can pray has nothing to fear because the person is safe in the presence of God. Challenges teach us two things; to remain faithful, and prayerful.

It is possible that, if you continue to keep your trust in God, obey the voice of the spirit then you will be getting close to your breakthrough.

To have God as your refuge and fortress, you must believe in His promises towards you. As long as God is our refuge does not mean that no danger will threaten and no harm will befall a believer.

And that does not also mean God will not intervene in our situations. God tells us through His Word that all who seek to live a godly life in Jesus Christ will be persecuted (2 Timothy 3:12).

The persecution may last for a while thereafter is going to be the joy of the Lord. Having trust in God is what we all need to survive in our present challenges.

We need faith to possess our possession, fight life's battles and achieve what God has destined for us.

In this way, God led the Israelites into battles against armies much more powerful than they, yet when they trusted God and obeyed Him, they always came out victorious.

Jesus told us, **"In me, you may have peace. In this world, you will have trouble. But take heart! I have overcome the world"** (John 16:33).

A simple declaration of Psalm 91:2 causes a lot of confusion and frustration for the devil. Because instead of them to see you crying, you are rejoicing.

Instead of them to see you weeping, you are seen singing and dancing to the King of Kings and Lord of Lords.

That verse " my God; in him will I trust" gives you confidence that what was impossible for others is going to be possible with you.

All things are possible with your overcoming faith today. God works all things together for the good of the believer.

That ultimate good is our conformity to the image of Christ and eternal life with God (Romans 8:28–30).

With that in mind, you will end up saying my God is my refuge and fortress.

One way of seeing God being our refuge ad fortress is how he protects us through sleeping, our going out and coming in.

Our salvation is guaranteed by Him, and He is also faithful to work in our lives to remove the power sin has over us.

He sets us free from bondage to sin and binds us to Himself and His righteousness (Romans 6:16–23; Galatians 5:1).

In a bid to fulfill destiny, people often realize that God is unjust to them. They believe God is keeping many miles away from them. They believe nothing good will ever be heard from them.

Every day, they lost hope to the devil. The Bible says, **Submit yourselves therefore to God. Resist the devil, and he will flee from you"** (James 4:7).

TAKE THE FOLLOWING PRAYERS:

- Lord makes an end of every demonic squad raised against my life and destiny, in Jesus' name.
- Father God destroy by fire all sorcerers attacking my interests in Jesus' name.
- My Father and God, make an end of the terror by night delegated against me, in the name of Jesus.
- Lord, make an end of all counterfeit angels working against my life and destiny, in Jesus name
- Lord, Make an end of the destruction that walks in the darkness assigned against me, in Jesus' name.

CHAPTER FIVE

THE SNARE OF THE FOWLER

Psalm 91:3, **"Surely he shall deliver thee from the snare of the fowler, and from the noisome pestilence."**

The fowler is a hunter, who pursues and eagerly follow after its prey. The agenda of the fowlers is to trap, eliminate, kill, ridicule, wound, capture and degrade.

The fowler's snare is a trap laid by a hunter to catch a bird. It is often hidden from the sight of the bird. In the spiritual realm, the fowler represents the devil.

One of his missions is to set a snare for the children of God in order to arrest and lock them up in a cage. While the Psalmist also mentions "noisome pestilence", which refers to deadly diseases.

However, If anyone can deliver us from deadly pestilences, it is the Lord our God. This verse does not mean that all those who trust in God will never die of diseases or encounter tough challenges. But rather,

He will deliver us from such troubles until our work on earth is done or perfected.

The snare of the fowler is all around us. They come in various forms. They can wait patiently for a long time to catch their victims. They are usually hidden and not exposed.

They are often set by close enemies, people that are very close to you. For example, your spouse can set a trap for you.

Your co-worker can set a spiritual net for you in the areas of cobwebs, nightmares and bad associates. They are set to catch you at your unguarded moments.

It could be to destroy various areas of your life including your soul, potentials, talents, virtues, anointing, health, wealth, relationships, marriage, opportunity, and ministry. The fowler normally puts a piece of food or something to attract the victim.

A good example is a trap that was set for Samson in the Bible using his weakness for the strange women. Judges 14:1-3.

He fell into the trap through Delilah and this led to his untimely death with his enemies. Judges 19-30.

That will not be our portion in Jesus' name. In some cases, the snare of a fowler" could also refer to a false prophet, a corrupt prophet, who attempts to lead God's people astray.

The Bible warns us of false prophets, false teachers, crafty people who hide under the name of a church or anointing to defraud or to catch their gullible members. The story of Gehazi as the snare of the fowler using the name of the prophet (Elisha) to collect the prophet offerings. (2 Kings 5:20-27).

In life, we must be very careful of a certain set of people we felt might not have the boldness to do us any harm now or in the near future.

In several places, the Bible tells us the best way to deal with our enemies is through prayers and fasting (Isaiah 58:6).

The Bible says it is very possible for an ancient snare can be broken and our soul can totally escape.

I pray that in any way your soul has been tied by the snare of the devil, the power of the Holy Spirit will destroy the yoke in Jesus' name.

One of the strongest keys to victory from spiritual bondage is the ability to determine the strengths and weaknesses of the fowler and strike against them.

 The truth is until you disgrace the fowler, they will keep disgracing you. The founder of strange sicknesses and diseases upon the children of God is from the fowler who has successfully set a net for their unwise victims.

It is a bad thing for the enemy to arrest and place you in their custody for long. When you discover you are trapped by a strongman, many things go wrong.

So, in the scriptures, the Bible says, for wrestle not against flesh and blood, but against principalities and powers.

These powers tormenting your life and hindering your moving progress has to be brought down today.

The earlier you loose yourself from their snares, the better it is for your freedom. As a child of God, you need to know the type of snares that have limited you.

Is it a snare of the marital embargo, a snare of lifetime battles, a snare of 10 times backward, a snare of losing your precious opportunities?

Oftentimes, so many people, including parents issues powerful curses to work against a certain person's destiny.

There are some curses that will not take immediate effects until a certain period of time. It is possible to notice a person under the snare of the fowler.

The devil will make it difficult for their victims to achieve good things if at all they are still getting their act together.

Ordinary to get a reward from his sweat becomes in vain. When you struggle to get things done when others do it with ease, then you are under the control of the snare of the fowler.

When you notice that you want to move forward and something keeps drawing you back then it tells you that part of your original have been tied down by the enemy.

The major challenge of Christians today is ignorance, not even prayerlessness. They continue to eat and dine with their enemy.

 They continue to distribute divine ideas, a revelation to the enemies.

Perhaps you had a dream where a personality caged your hands and legs. Or you simply got a revelation about an animal been tied down know that you are under the control and manipulation of witchcraft household agents.

The fowlers are very good looking, but inwardly, they know they are after you. That's why Christians need to be more prayerful in an aggressive way.

 Honestly, if we the way people are praying are the most accepted, there would have been massive deliverance. Many people just take their Bible and read the book of Psalm 91 without necessarily having to know what it actually meant in the first place.

Reading the Bible is good, but what are the benefits of reading without studying it. It is good to pray for the Psalmist prayers of protection before bedtime. It is also good to take the psalmist prayers to charge the angel of God to encamped you while asleep.

It is also good to take psalm prayer that every night evil arrows should go back to the senders. It is very possible both in the physical and spiritual realm for your husband or wife to be the fowler of your progress and restoration.

The total deliverance from the snare of the Fowler and noisome pestilence is becoming harder. The stubbornness of the wicked makes a prayer to go unanswered.

 God does not expect His children to be candidates of the valley of stagnation and limitation.

He expects them to break grounds and perform great exploits.

The snare of the fowler can possibly affect a person's health. When a person's health is caged, the person begins to use the money to maintain his sickness that defies medical solutions.

It may also be a ministry. The ministry is making progress but alongside heaven does not satisfy with the rate of the slow pace of the movement.

It may affect a person in his academics. He is making progress, but it is little progress. It may be a person in his job. Everybody else is being promoted and given a salary increase, but his own will never be commensurate with his qualifications.

 Why? There may be a spiritual cage over his life. What the enemy does to a caged individual is to draw a spiritual circle around him.

He is only allowed to operate within that circle. Every blessing outside that circle is kept out of his reach. There are some things happening to people that is beyond one's understanding. So, no one can explain the genesis of his problems.

If you discover the fowler has adopted several methods of putting your destiny in a bottle, then you must be ready to pray your way to your breakthrough.

The purpose of the demonic snare is to say, "you can go this far but no farther. You can get that job or marry the person but you will not enjoy his fruitfulness" That is why you see some men and women, no matter how hard they try, they can only achieve up to a point.

All efforts after that point end in frustration. May that not be your portion in Jesus name.

TAKE THE FOLLOWING PRAYERS:

- I pursue, overtake and recover my glory from the hands of spiritual robbers, in the name of Jesus.
- Let every counsel, plan, desire, expectation, imagination, device and activity of the oppressors against my life be rendered null and void, in the name of Jesus.

- I terminate every contract and cancel every evil promissory note kept in satanic files for my sake, in the name of Jesus.
- I release myself form the powers and activities of the wasters, in the name of Jesus.
- I push the enemy inside the grave dug for me, in the name of Jesus.
- I push the enemy inside the coffin made for me, in the name of Jesus.
- Blood of Jesus bring law and order into every area of my life under chaos, in the name of Jesus.

CHAPTER 6

HIS FEATHERS AND WINGS

Psalm 91:4, **"He shall cover thee with his feathers, and under his wings shalt thou trust: his truth shall be thy shield and buckler."**

The image of God "[covering] us with his feathers" in Psalm 91:4 and in other Bible passages (see Psalm 17:8) is one of comfort and protection.

The image that comes to mind is a mother bird covering her little ones with her feathers. Jesus refers to this image as he looked over Jerusalem (Matthew 23:37; Luke 13:34).

Bird feathers are an amazing example of God's design for Psalm 91:4. Like a hen who baby roosters from a hawk, that's the place of God in our lives.

We must understand the good plans of heavens towards us. The plan of protection and security of life and properties.

When the Bible says, He shall cover you with his feather and under his wings shall thou trust means that God will protect you from everything that portend fear and threat to you.

 Fear has no place in the heart or mind of a believer. Ask God to increase your trust and faith in his willingness and ability to deliver you completely from fear and anxiety.

God promised protection and deliverance to Menshack, Shadrach, and Abednego when they entered into the fire.

When King Nebuchadnezzar looked into the fire he saw four men walking around in the furnace unharmed and promoted them to a higher office and decreed that the God of Israel be worshipped.

That's the God of the feather of protection. Many times God sends angels to protect, guard, and fight for us.

The Bible says in Psalm 91 that He would give angels charge concerning us to guard us in all our ways. God covered Daniel in the lion's den with his feather.

Daniel 6:22 says that he shut the mouth of the lions so that no harm came to him who was found blameless before God. God's feathers and wings are not literal obviously but show that He will protect us like a hen protecting her chicks, hiding them under her wings.

If we have this protection, why then do we need a shield? It's even listed in the armor of God.

In 2 Kings 19, King Hezekiah prayed boldly to God, asking for his help against their enemies. The Assyrians were known for the cruel way they treated their captives. Verse 35 says, "That night, the angel of the Lord went out and put to death a hundred and eighty-five thousand men..."

 Feather and wings go together. When God's angels come to you in the form of a bird, his mission is to take over your battles and declare war against the enemies of your destiny fulfillment.

The Bible says, his truth shall be thy shield and buckler meaning that the word of God is our shield.

Furthermore, a shield is important to a soldier going into war. It provides a blanket of protection and defense. It is the first barrier against the enemy's attack.

When the Bible says, he will be our shield and buckler can also be put as the angels of war are there fighting for us and we shall hold our peace. (Exodus 14:14).

God is a fighter. It is a thing of joy for God to fight your battles. The book of Psalms 119:89 says **"Forever, O LORD, Your word is settled in heaven."**

The Word of God is the only source for absolute divine authority and power. This divine authority is for you. The word of God cannot lie.

When he says, His word is your shield believe it is so in your life. For example, if God told you something will do something, and you wait, it will happen or come to pass.

In Isaiah 55:11 it says, **"So shall My word be that goes forth from My mouth; It shall not return to Me void, But it shall accomplish what I please,**

And it shall prosper in the thing for which I sent it."

God sent His word to accomplish His perfect will in our lives. If God makes a promise to you He will fulfill it in His own time. If God says, go, for I am with you. Please go, and never look back.

The problem of many is faith issues. The level of faith attaches to our prayer is low. Hence, most people resort to the service of false priests all in the name of fast miracle.

Nobody can give you maximum protection except the King of Kings. Is your life troubled day by day?

The messiah is around to calm the storm in your life.

TAKE THE FOLLOWING PRAYERS:

- By fire, by force, I push my enemies inside the coffin they manufactured for me this year, in the name of Jesus.

- Every satanic image set up to bewitch my life through occultism and magic, I damage you, in the name of Jesus.
- I command satanic missiles to be redirected and to backfire, in the name of Jesus.
- I smash every negative prayer put upon me by any dark personality, in the name of Jesus.
- I destroy every curse targeted against me from the covens, in the name of Jesus.
- Every power of the shadow of death over my destiny, break, in the name of Jesus.

CHAPTER 7

I SHALL NOT BE AFRAID

Psalm 91:5, **"Thou shalt not be afraid for the terror by night; nor for the arrow that flieth by day;"**

This is a verse that every believer should memorize. This is one of the best Psalmists that you should be said mostly at night before bedtime.

Among many other things, the power of God upon this verse is enough to give you boldness and build your confidence against any evil assigned to befall you or any of your loved ones.

God's plan and purpose for the righteous are to save them from trouble. The word of God has very bad news for the wicked.

Let us look at some of them. Job 8:22 says, **"They that hate thee shall be clothed with shame, and the dwelling place of the wicked shall come to naught."**

The Bible says that the dark place of the world is full of the habitation of wickedness and that wickedness shall increase.

It did not say it will reduce. Thou shall not be afraid for the terror by night, the Bible makes us understand here that, though there will be troubles that will bring you down, do not be afraid of them.

It went further to say, nor for the arrow that flieth by day, this also means that at any time you should not be afraid of the advances of the enemy.

When they attack you, then use the word of God to attack them. That's what the Psalmist is saying here. The life of a Christian is known for winning battles of the day and night. There is no particular time for prayers.

Because the devil may strike at you at your unguarded hour. The rate of spiritual attacks is getting too much and most believers are becoming frustrated.

For example, when somebody dreams that a snake bit him, what can that mean? It means the grip of the marine witchcraft over his life and destiny.

The person wakes up to find out that he is losing things, he is not prosperous again. In the realm of the spirit, people send snakes to people. Sometimes, I pity those who don't pray at all.

What Psalm 91:5 is telling us is that we are fully under divine protection through victory in the blood of Jesus.

Prayer in the scripture is very effective and eye-opening. Even though you don't know the kind of prayer to pray, or you are simply lazy to drag your mouth to pray.

Just read and recite Psalm 91 into your spirit. It helps. When you are under God's protection, you have no reason to fear.

When you are under God's eyes, no powers can invade into your life. The wicked loves believers that don't pray. Satanic agents work better in darkness to perpetuate their witchcraft manipulation.

The devil has no good agenda, but to steal, kill and destroy. The Psalms of David are filled with warfare prayers as He protected His chosen one against his enemies (Psalm 18:3, 54:7, 138:7).

No matter the amount of power or wrath that David's enemies brought against him, they were no able to match for the protection of God.

A man who is fervent in prayers, soaked in tongues cannot be afraid for the terror by night. A man who has the apostolic vision to bring billions of souls to God's kingdom shall not be afraid of what the devil can do to him.

A man who went to a village to conduct family liberation will never be afraid of demonic reinforcement.

God has several ways of protecting his children from early destruction and death. The arrow of the day that flieth by day is different from the attack that flieth by night.

Every arrow has several purposes that influence people under the surveillance of the wicked. God can make sure none of the arrows touch you. He has promised your safety in his word (Isaiah 41:10).

Once the enemy knows that you are untouchable, perhaps they have seen an invisible arm covering you, they will begin to lose their attention on you.

I pray for you, any book of death opened unto you shall be destroyed, in Jesus' name.

For record purposes, there are some arrows of the day fired into the lives of most people.

These include:

- Arrows of get and loose.
- Arrow of depression and frustration.
- Arrow of bad luck and losses.
- Arrow of marital troubles.
- Arrow of joblessness and errors.
- Arrow of near success syndrome.
- Arrow of lifetime battles and afflictions.

Some arrows sent into people's life by night.

These include:

- Arrows of untimely death.
- Arrows of sickness that defies medical treatment.
- Arrow of losing your investments and aborted expectations. Arrows of sleeping more than normal.
- Witchcraft arrows of conflict between married couples. Household arrows of barrenness and miscarriage.
- Stubborn arrows of quality poverty and fruitless efforts.

TAKE THE FOLLOWING PRAYERS:

- I dissolve every link and connection between my life and any ancestral iniquity, in the name of Jesus.
- God, arise and send Your angels to bind the strongmen carrying out witchcraft errands in my family line, in the name of Jesus.
- By the power in the blood of Jesus, let every injury done to me physically

and spiritually be reversed, in Jesus' name.

- I cancel any bewitchment of any photograph or image that has ever be created for me, in the name of Jesus.
- heavens, arise with the light of God and put to shame every power assigned to put me to shame, in the name of Jesus.

CHAPTER 8

PROTECTION OVER PESTILENCE

Psalm 91:6, **"Nor for the pestilence that walketh in darkness; nor for the destruction that wasteth at noonday."**

Pestilence is an infectious and deadly disease (tragedy) that affects an entire community.

A disease that causes widespread crop damage or animal deaths can also be called a pestilence. In some countries, perhaps, Nigeria, the new pestilence that floods some states is Lassa Fever.

It is reported that Lassa fever is an acute, viral disease carried by a type of rat that is common in West Africa.

It can be life-threatening. It begins from a mild to severe epidemic to a community. Presently we are experiencing a global pestilence and plague called coronavirus.

Pestilence is typically a contagious disease, in the Biblical accounts, it is a judgment of God on a particular group of people.

"They have blown the trumpet, even to make all ready; but none goeth to the battle: for my wrath is upon all the multitude thereof.

The sword is without, and the pestilence and the famine within: he that is in the field shall die with the sword, and he that is in the city, famine and pestilence shall devour him." Ezekiel 7:14-15.

The arrow of the disease can be brought about when an individual is possessed, oppressed, or is in rebellion towards God (sins of the flesh).

The Bible makes it clear that there are diseases satanically influenced to punish a person. So, the confession of Psalm 91:6 is a true confirmation that you are prevented from sickness unto death.

In any pestilence, death is inevitable. Throughout the Scriptures, good health, either in a physical or in a spiritual sense, is associated with God's blessing (Deuteronomy 7:12, 15; Psalm 103:1-3), whereas disease is associated with sin and imperfection. (Exodus 15:26; Deuteronomy 28:58-61; Isaiah 53:4, 5).

Not every disease that struck so many people are actually from Satan, majorly from God. But the Bible says He will take the diseases which he has brought to the land of Egypt. (Deuteronomy 7:15).

The above verse is a fact that God has protected us from the contamination of infectious diseases. Though, He does not want us to die and perish in sickness and diseases.

The constant confession of the above verse can bring about divine healing and build a divine immunity in you against any external diseases that may want to threaten you to death.

God knows that there are going to diseases that destroy people at their unguarded hour. As long you as you are a believer, nothing shall harm you.

Psalm 91 is a powerful chapter that encourages believers to pray and praise God.

However, If you want to pray a prayer of protection, Psalm 91 is a good place to start. For those who believe in the book of Psalm for prayers, I would say you are denying yourself of divine protection and care.

It is a waste of time hiding your Bible under your pillow or placing your Bible at the entrance of your door. That can't restrict the devil from attacking you.

Maybe your proceed was picked from a movie. Learn to pray using Psalm 91, but if the word of God says none of the destruction will come near your dwelling shows the love of God towards you. Some miracles don't come except you pray.

Some healing doesn't manifest until you hold unto the word of God for your healing. From the scripture, it is understood that God can use His angels to save us from future deadly evil attacks.

The moment you are under God's arm, you will be prevented from experiencing sorrow and weeping. Some people don't believe in the word of God no matter your preaching to them.

They will rather do what's in their mind. However, if you believe the word of God is what you need to come out from the shackles of the devil then it will save you. Learn to personalize the prophecies.

TAKE THE FOLLOWING PRAYERS:

- Lord, by the power in your name, I stand against and scatter every plan of the devil and its cohort to oppose your plans in my life today, in Jesus Christ name.
- I scatter every written plan of the devil and its cohort against my marriage and my children today, in Jesus Christ name.
- I send back to the pit of hell every demonic agent on assignment against my progress and prosperity in life today in Jesus Christ name.
- Dear heavenly father, help me to know how to spend my money wisely and not to be a miser, in Jesus Christ powerful name.

- I rebuke every devourer that might want to devour my finances today in Jesus Christ name.

CHAPTER 9

EVIL SHALL NOT LOCATE ME

Psalm 91:7, **"A thousand shall fall at thy side, and ten thousand at thy right hand; but it shall not come to nigh thee."**

This is one of the strongest and popular verses of Psalm 91. Psalm 91:7 explains the reasons why evil will not locate you.

A thousand shall fall at thy side and ten thousand at thy right hand are ironically words that symbolize troubles, problems, satanic oppression, calamity, etc, But the Bible all these negative spirits will ever have the chance to attack you.

In God, we children of God are boast of His divine protection. But when the faith is not falling apart, the ten thousand and others begin to tear us apart from left to right, front and back.

The Bible stretches this in the book of Isaiah 54:17 says, **"No weapon that is formed against thee shall prosper, and every tongue that shall rise up against**

thee in judgment thou shalt condemn. This is the heritage of the servants of the Lord and their righteousness is of me, saith the Lord."

The above verse is telling us that there are wasters. The agenda of the wasters are:

- To render something worthless or to make it useless.
- To damage something completely and to hijack and steal away something precious from you.

Looking at Psalm 91 prayer of protection: A lot of people are being wasted every day because they never find out the causes giving ways for such an attack.

The devil finishes most people completely by making them hold a statement of "I have prayed, and fasted, nothing happened.

I have done so many deliverance. There is no sign of miracle and wonders. Every day, they give themselves to the devil all in the name of a fast miracle.

Our God understands the daily afflictions of many and that's why He used David to put down the Psalmist for our benefits.

The Bible says, Thousands will be dying, but the protected will not be touched. Thousand will be weeping, but you will not be affected. The disaster or strong attack is close, but those hidden in the Lord are not affected.

This could be a horrific plague or possibly a weapon of mass destruction. Nearly everyone in the family is affected by the inherited problems, but the Bible says, it shall not come near you. Many will be jumping from one challenge to the other.

The Bible says, he will make your way out. It is humanly impossible to survive the arrow of death and sickness.

No matter their wicked act, the wickedness of the wicked shall be terminated. "At thy side…at thy right hand..but it shall not come nigh thee."

This appears to be a warning as it sounds like the advance of the wicked is indeed very close. It will appear to be close, but it will not touch you or any of your family if you are abiding in the secret place of the Almighty.

God will not allow it to happen to you. You will be surrounded by it on every side, but not be affected by it. It will not touch you because God stands between it and you if you are dwelling in the secret place.

The Bible verses make us understand the mysterious operation of the wicked. The enemy who steals your money will surely prevent you from having a financial breakthrough.

The enemy who went to a herbalist to lock up your blessings does not want you to celebrate.

The beauty of Psalm 91 is a timely and wonderful statement for those believers who simply don't joke with prayers of Psalmist.

Obviously, if you want to enjoy your life and fulfill your destiny, you must be reading and reciting the book of Psalm 91:1-16.

It will surely help you to overcome some battles of life. That's why you must allow the words to be sound in your spirit at all time so that you can come out and say with full confidence: "There is nothing the devil can do to me, From henceforth, no man trouble me, for I bear in my body the mark of Christ."

May evil never see you, in Jesus name.

TAKE THE FOLLOWING PRAYERS:

- Father, I bring myself into your secret place and under your shadow this day, in Jesus' name.
- Father, I declare today that you are my refuge and my fortress, in Jesus' Name.
- I shield myself today from the terrors of the night, in Jesus name
- Every demonic attack sent against me in the night shall backfire by fire, in Jesus name
- Every evil gang up or conspiracy and gang up against me is rendered null and void, in Jesus name.

CHAPTER 10

DIVINE HABITATION

Psalm 91:8-9, **"Only with thine eyes shalt thou behold and see the reward of the wicked. Because thou hast made the Lord, which is my refuge, even the most High, thy habitation."**

There is the wickedness of the wicked everywhere. Many people are suffering from the daily torment of the wicked. Those who are not under the protective hedge of the Almighty God are the ones been affected by the arrows of the devil.

Many people tear down the hedge of protection that God built around them with their mouth and sin.

In the verse above, the Bible is saying that God's judgment placed on the wicked will not touch the righteous and that you will only see it on others.

This is a true confirmation of God's plan for your life in Psalm 23:4, **"Yea, though I walk through the valley of the shadow of death, I will fear no evil: for thou art**

with me; thy rod and thy staff they comfort me."

This means that the plans of the enemies will not catch up with you. And even though they set a trap for you, it will not catch you.

Psalm 91:8 makes us understand that those who speak evil things against you shall be punished for it.

In verse 9, when the Lord is your refuge, there is bound to be testimony, mercy, and peace of mind. Perhaps as you are reading this, you find out that you are not safe, then you need to pray.

The moment you find it difficult to have good sleep at night, then it shows that your enemies are after you or they are troubling your life.

When God is not with you, you are bound to fall into divers temptation and troubles set out for you by the enemies.

How can you say God should protect you when you are dealing with fetish things?

How can you say evil should not locate you when you are the evil of yourself?

How can you say God should protect you when you are a friend of a false priest?

It is very common to experience to see lots of believers running from one church to another seeking for a solution.

The truth is, if you are not in good standing with God, you will be troubled. Perhaps you did an abortion.

Maybe you used someone for rituals purposes. Then the meaning of the above verses shows that God's judgment will bounce on you.

Many believers have not realized the punishment of God. When you take the word of God for a joke, you begin to drain away.

Do you know that there are some people in the face of the planet they don't sleep the way I and you do?

This life is a mystery. The word of God has come to refuge us from daily calamities. On the other hand, if you are a righteous person, the Bible says, only with your eyes thou shall the punishment of the wicked.

This literally means a bundle of testimonies. For many people, reading Psalm 91 is a daily practice because of the degree of their challenges.

You're reading this because you want God to save you. You 're reading this because you are being arrested and dump in satanic captivity. You are reading this because all the days of your life are sorrow and weeping.

The blessings of God upon Psalm 91 will make a way for you and stand as a shield to you. Jesus is the protective arm of God that saves people from the hands of the enemy.

The recitation of the Psalmist prayers puts an end to all pain, all suffering, all disappointment, poverty, failures, battles, sorrows, etc. For those who trust in the Lord shall not end up in shame.

In that same Psalm 91-9, explains the habitation, which indicates where you stay, finds comfort, goes for safety, returns for rest, and stays for pleasure.

Because thou hast made the Lord, which is my refuge, even the most High, thy habitation; This also means that, in God, there is no more suffering and manipulation of the wicked. God is the habitation of his people, who find rest and safety in him (Psalms 71:3 ; 91:9).

In this scripture, our God created a place in his heart for us to dwell in.

Many people have chosen men as their own form of habitation and refuge. How wrong they are. They hired some prophets to be praying for them in the areas of protection.

These men have continued to deceive them by extorting their hard-earned money. In the process, some people have contacted the wrong anointing and for this purpose, and that's the reason evils are befalling them.

More so, The powers of sin have made people give up in the place of prayers when they have temporary setbacks. Such people just move through life without divine protection from evil attacks.

It is unfortunate. There are some people who go through life expecting God to be their refuge and if God did not intervene, they say, I am an unfortunate being to God.

These people end up blaming others for their predicaments when they should have remained steadfast in the Lord. The truth is, if you don't believe what God will do, His grace and help will not come.

TAKE THE FOLLOWING PRAYERS:

- I shield myself from every arrow that flies by day in Jesus' name.
- Every demonic agent sending arrows to me by day shall return back to the sender in Jesus' name.
- Every arrow of stagnation shall return back to the sender in Jesus' name.
- Every arrow of untimely death shall return back to the sender in Jesus' name.

- Every arrow of marital stagnation shall return back to the sender in Jesus' name.

CHAPTER 11

NO EVIL SHALL BEFALL ME

Psalm 91:10-11 **''There shall no evil befall thee, neither shall any plague come to nigh thy dwelling. For he shall give his angels charge over thee, to keep thee in all thy ways.''**

This is the prayer of the Psalmist towards the righteous.

As a child of God, it is very important to know that no evil shall befall you. It is very important to believe that the angels of God are with you.

It is very good to have the belief that you are not going to end in shame and disgrace. So, let that confession remains with you now and forever.

In addition, this verse is powered by God to work against fear and insecurity. In the scripture, there shall no evil befall you neither shall any plague come near your dwelling means the spirit of darkness has no right to steal your joy.

It means you are God's anointed child. What happens when the enemy tries to lay his evil hands on you, the power of God upon your life will roast them to ashes.

More importantly, remind God all the time through His words in Psalm 138:7, "Though I walk in the midst of trouble, You will revive me; You will stretch out Your hand against the wrath of my enemies, and Your right hand will save me."

As a child of God, are you afraid to take the prayer of the Psalmist?

Are you feeling like you are unsafe or soaked in affliction? Fear not, the word of God will deliver you today. Please note that the presence of the Holy Spirit with you is proof that you belong to God.

He has sent His angel to guide and protect you from demonic attacks. Also, if you are in Christ Jesus, the present battles are not forever, they are possible manifesting for a short moment.

Be strong and do not fear. The Bible commands us to pray always, not only occasionally. God wants to pray more in order to send his angels to take charge and keep all through our life.

Take authority over and all principalities and powers and that act would make your enemies uncomfortable. This means the more you bind and cast them out, the weaker they become.

Taking the prayer of protection can seem like heaven is not in concern. However, if you take it one step at a time and praying it aggressively, you'll soon be a happy person. Before you begin prophesying Psalm 91 into your life, check yourself very well.

Make sure you have taken your time to repent and confess your sin. In the Bible, Micah saw heaven opened and all the host of heaven awaiting their orders (I Kings 22:19-23).

Elisha asked God to open the eyes of His servant to see the protecting host (II Kings 6:16-17).

It is very unfortunate that many have eyes but could not see the movement of God towards them. They made several complains to God that He hasn't done so much for them.

They conclude that so many things are falling apart without divine intervention and help. When we sleep, we complain that our sleep is bad.

When we find ourselves in an organization, we complain of gang up attacks. When we receive blessings from God, we complain too much. The essence of the above verse is telling you about God's love.

It is telling you that there is going to be a new beginning. It is telling you of maximum divine protection. Perhaps you woke up in the middle of the night crying out for help.

You were attacked in the head, hands, legs. Or you felt your virtue has gone out of you.

The Bible says, Jeremiah 29:12-13, "**Then shall ye call upon me, and ye shall go and pray unto me, and I will hearken unto you. And ye shall seek me, and find me when ye shall search for me with all your heart.**"

In the verse above, when the angels of God take charge of you and keep you in all thy ways, it speaks more of protection and divine intervention.

It means the angels of God shall have an especial charge to accompany, defend, and preserve thee; and against their power.

The angels of God moving and covering the life of the righteous. His presence in our life is enough to remove the seed of anxiety and depression in our lives.

TAKE THE FOLLOWING PRAYERS:

- I shield myself from every destruction that attacks at noonday in Jesus' name.
- I release the angels of the Lord to go ahead of me day to day, to shield me from every form of destruction in Jesus name.
- Lord, liberate my spirit to follow the leading of the Holy Spirit.
- Lord, increase my spiritual sensitivity, in the name of Jesus.

- Lord, deliver me from the lies I tell to myself, in Jesus' name.
- Every evil spiritual padlock and evil chain, hindering my success, roast, in the name of Jesus.
- I rebuke every spirit of spiritual deafness and blindness in my life, in the name of Jesus.
- Lord, empower me to resist Satan so that he would flee from me.

CHAPTER 12

ANGELS TAKE CHARGE

Psalm 91:12-13 **''They shall bear thee up in their hands, lest thou dash thy foot against a stone. Thou shalt tread upon the lion and adder: the young lion and the dragon shalt thou trample under feet.''**

In the Scripture, God sent angels to Sodom to deliver Lot for the righteous Abraham (Genesis 18:20-33; 19:1-23).

He sent an angel to deliver Hezekiah that killed 185,000 Assyrians in one night (II Kings 19:35).

God sent an angel to deliver the three men from Nebuchadnezzar's fiery furnace (Daniel 3:28).

God sent an angel to deliver Daniel from hungry lions in the lions' den of Persia (Daniel 6:22).

God sent angels to comfort our Lord Jesus Christ after being tempted by the devil (Matthew 4:11).

God sent an angel to comfort the Lord Jesus Christ in the Garden of Gethsemane (Luke 22:43).

God sent an angel to deliver Peter from prison when Herod intended his death (Acts 12:5-11).

According to the Bible verse, it is possible as a child of God for evil to keep a distance from you. It is possible for you to walk in the midst of trouble and the challenges will not swallow up your hopes and faith.

Also, it is possible according to Psalm 121:7-8 **"for The LORD will keep you from all harm and watches over your life."**

 The Bible says he has given you the power to tread upon serpent and scorpions. This means that God has empowered or given you a license of destruction over the enemy.

When the LORD says you shall tread upon the enemy and adder then it automatically symbolizes divine protection and helps.

Our God fully understands the purpose of the devil and what they can do to make their victims cry and perish.

The Bible shows that God pays special attention to our safety. He does not want us to be defeated by witchcraft. He does not want the enemy to ride on our horses. He does not want the devil to take the glory.

If you read your Bible from Genesis to Revelation, you will come to an agreement with me that God loves us with perfect love.

God promises for mankind: **"I will protect him because he knows my name. He will call on me, and I will answer him. I will be with him in distress."** (Psalm 91:14, 15).

 By definition, an adder is a poisonous snake; a young lion is very strong; a dragon is any very fierce creature. Also in the spirit realm, an adder could be referred to as a strongman.

A snake is a poisonous animal can endanger a person's relationship with God.

The moment the serpent bite you, what happens is, the hedge of protection is being lifted away from you.

I pray for you today, every of your divine garment of glory that has been taken away shall be restored to you, in Jesus' name.

If you're living with high levels of fear, there is no way you can tread on the serpent and its stronghold. The enemy of our soul can wreak havoc on our destiny, as well as our marriage.

But if we keep on having the grace to fight, pray and dismantle the host of witchcraft, there shall be outstanding victory and testimony. It is no longer enough to follow Church doctrine, Christians need full power to demonstrate the authority in the blood of Jesus.

To carry out the marching order in the scripture above, a higher power is needed and this power is the presence of God. When Ephesians 6:10 says "**Finally, be strong in the Lord and in his mighty power**" it implies a Christian can be

weak in the Lord and lacking in power.''

Only the power of God can confront serpents and overcome the power of the enemy so if you are not spiritually filled with God's power you cannot face and judge the serpents and your enemies.

You have to arise and fight your serpents by connecting to the power to tread upon. This power can be acquired by genuinely born again Christians who are living a holy life and have cried out to God to deposit this power in their lives.

Then when the power is in you, you can boldly speak death unto your own serpent with fire prayers and throw them into the fire just as Paul did on the island of Malta (Acts 28:1).

 May God protect you from the lion and the adder, in the name of Jesus.

TAKE THE FOLLOWING PRAYERS:

- You, the angel of protection, protect me and my family from the attack of the enemy, in the name of Jesus.
- You, the angel of my greatness; go to the heavenly, go to the water, go to the land, and fight for me, in the name of Jesus.
- You, the angel of my business; go and bring customers to me, in the name of Jesus.
- You, the angel of my healing; go and get my healing, in the name of Jesus.
- You, the angel of my deliverance; go and get my deliverance, in the name of Jesus.
- You, the angel of my marriage; go and get my marriage for me, in the name of Jesus.
- You, the angel of my ministry; go to the heavenly, go to the land, go to the water fight my battle for me, in the name of Jesus.
- You, my angel go to my office; write my name on the list of promotions, in the name of Jesus.

- You, my angel of financial abundance; go to the four corners of this world; go to the elements and bring me financial abundance, in the name of Jesus.
- All the good doors that are closed against me; be open by the angels of my breakthrough, in the name of Jesus.
- You, the angel of my divine upliftment; uplift me now, in the name of Jesus.
- You, the angels of God go and shut the mouth of the lions assigned to eat me up in my place of work, in the name of Jesus.
- You, the angels of God go and disorganize every evil meeting assigned against me, in the name of Jesus.
- Anything in my life; that will make me be a disgrace in the days of my honor. Thou angel of death, kill it, in the name of Jesus.

CHAPTER 13

LORD BLESS ME

Psalm 91:14-16, **"Because he hath set his love upon me, therefore will I deliver him: I will set him on high because he hath known my name. He shall call upon me, and I will answer him: I will be with him in trouble; I will deliver him, and honor him. With long life will I satisfy him, and shew him my salvation."**

These last three verses are set in the first person as God speaks promise and blessing over His people. He speaks specifically over those who set their love upon Him.

It has been wonderfully noted that the last words of this psalm are not spoken by God's people, but to God's people. In verse 14, There are two conditions here – setting your affection on God and knowing His glorious name.

Loving God is the first and great commandment; He demands and expects our first love. Knowing His name is much more than knowing it mentally, but rather loving and trusting it.

The condition, for evidence, for a crown of righteousness is based on loving Christ (II Timothy 4:8).

Do you know His name? Is it all your trust? Do you speak of it often with others (Malachi 3:16-18)?

God does not miss your treatment of Him or His name. He will reward all that worship Him. The importance of setting your love upon God was highlighted in one of Jesus' parables.

As Jesus proclaimed the good news throughout Palestine, crowds gathered to hear him. (Luke 8:1, 4) Not all, however, really loved God's Word. No doubt, many came to hear him because they wanted to see miracles or because they enjoyed his marvelous way of teaching.

The demonstration of verse 14 was said of the mission of Jesus into the earth.

The greatest expression of God's love is communicated to us in John 3:16: **"For**

God so loved the world that he gave his one and only Son, that whoever believes in him shall not perish but have eternal life."**

Romans 5:8 proclaims the same message: **"But God demonstrates his own love for us in this: While we were still sinners, Christ died for us."**

We can see from these verses that it is God's greatest desire that we join Him in His eternal home, heaven. He has made the way possible by paying the price for our sins.

He loves us because He chose to as an act of His will. Love forgives.

"If we confess our sins, he is faithful and just and will forgive us our sins and purify us from all unrighteousness" (1 John 1:9).

Love opens the window of deliverance and promotion. Everything God does is loving, just as everything He does is just and right.

So through these verses, he was to remain to look unto him as he makes plans to deliverance from the issues that limit us.

In verse 15, **"He shall call upon me, and I will answer him: I will be with him in trouble; I will deliver him, and honor him."**

 This means that the Lord hears the prayers of the righteous, but He does not hear the prayers of the wicked (Psalm 34:12-20; 66:18; 84:11; Proverbs 15:8; 28:9; John 9:31; I Peter 3:10-12; I John 3:22).

The above verse of the scriptures when we meditate on God's word in truth and in the right spirit, then the Holy Spirit promised to answer our petition as we render our spirit in high faith.

You can experience divine favor, divine blessings, divine health, and divine power. Jesus said, **"I have come that you might have life and have it more abundantly."** (John 10:10).

If you draw near to God and humble yourself before Him, He will lift you up (James 4:8-10).

It is God's will for you to live an abundant life full of His blessings. God is no respecter of persons.

What He has done in the lives of others He will surely do for you.

In verse 16, **"With long life will I satisfy him, and shew him my salvation."**

The truth is, God wants you to live long in good health and prosperity. God wants you to live more years to discover your gifts, break boundaries and fulfill your destiny.

God does not wish anyone death. In fact, God has several good plans for us. God does not only wants to give you a long life, but he also wants to give you a satisfying long life and show you His salvation, which is found in Christ.

Don't ever believe the devil's lie that God wants you to die an early death. Stand firm on the truth of God's Word, which says that He will satisfy you with long life. Believe it!

If others are dying untimely, whether in your family or elsewhere, the Bible says, I, Joshua, (personalize it) will not die but live to declare the works of God. For this reason, if any prophet sees a vision about you and tells you that you are going to die soon.

Reject it immediately. The moment you are given to fear, automatically you have signed a death agreement with death and hell.

May that not be your portion, in Jesus' name.

As long as you are fully alive, you have been satisfied with a long life.

Maybe you are currently battling with a terminal illness, the Bible says, he has satisfied you with long life which means the power of death over you has been destroyed by the blood of the lamb, in the name of Jesus (Revelations 12:11).

TAKE THE FOLLOWING PRAYERS:

- I chose to believe the report of the Lord and no other, in the name of Jesus.
- Lord, anoint my eyes and my ears so that they may see and hear wondrous things from heaven in Jesus' name.
- I frustrate every evil exchange of my virtues, in the name of Jesus.
- Blood of Jesus, block the flying route of evil powers, targeted at me.
- Every witchcraft curse, break and be destroyed, in Jesus' name.
- Every covenant of witchcraft, melt by the blood of Jesus.
- I withdraw every organ of my body from any witchcraft altar, in the name of Jesus.
- Anything planted in my life by the enemy, come out now and die, in the name of Jesus.
- Blood of Jesus, cancel every satanic initiation, fashioned against my destiny, in the name of Jesus.
- Every witchcraft poison, be destroyed, in the name of Jesus.

- I reverse every witchcraft pattern, fashioned against my destiny, in the name of Jesus.
- Every witchcraft cage, fashioned against my life, be destroyed, in the name of Jesus.
- Every problem in my life, that originated from witchcraft, receive the divine and instant solution, in Jesus' name.
- All the damages done to my life by witchcraft, be repaired, in the name of Jesus.
- Every blessing, confiscated by witchcraft spirits, be released, in Jesus' name.
- Every witchcraft power, assigned against my life and marriage, be destroyed in Jesus' name.
- I loose myself from any power of witchcraft, in Jesus' name.
- Every camp of witchcraft, gathered against my prosperity, fall down and die, in Jesus' name.
- Every witchcraft pot, working against me, I bring the judgment of God upon you, in the name of Jesus.

- Every witchcraft pot, using remote control against my health, break into pieces, in Jesus' name.
- Witchcraft opposition, receive the rain of affliction, in the name of Jesus.
- Spirit of witchcraft, attack the familiar spirits fashioned against me, in Jesus' name.
- O Lord, protect and bless the work of my hands, in Jesus name.

ABOUT THE BOOK

The Bible is the only weapon in which believers use to fight and proclaim formidable victory over the enemies.

Without the Bible, there can never be victory and our prayers become useless and the devil would begin to take the glory.

One of the powerful scriptures against night raiders, spiritual attacks and prayers that guarantee a peaceful sleep, is a prayer from the book of Psalm 91.

This psalm 91 prayer points for protection, will help you as you prayerfully build a wall of protection over your life.

ABOUT THE AUTHOR

Grace Remmy is a simple woman and a dedicated wife, who has discovered God's amazing gift of prayer.

In this book, I share my journey of unwrapping this powerful gift of prayer. God invites us to ask Him, but His enemy works diligently to keep that from happening.

I hope to offer you encouragement to believe God is ready to pour more into your life than you've ever imaged.

OTHER BOOKS BY THE AUTHOR

Prophetic Prayers for Children from A Loving Mother.